Flowers

From

My

Heart

K.J. Bashford

ISBN: 9781723712586

Dedicated to my grandmother, who taught me that writing comes from the roots of the heart.

Cover illustration by: K.J. Bashford

Cover design by: Kaitlyn Barone

CONTENTS

My inspiration resides from my imagination.

Some pieces in this collection relate to real life events.

My heart and soul were carefully poured into each of these poems.

Read them carefully, as you now hold a piece of my heart in your hands.

Thank you.

-K.J. Bashford

You picked apart the flowers from my heart

petal by petal

leaf by leaf

each one so fragile, yet greatly damaged

these tiny flowers represented me

they were a part of my soul, grown from seed to seed

they helped me stand tall, showed all my colors and let me be free

my flowers started to die as they were tampered with

left out in the hot sun to become dry and brittle

a drop of water was all you gave me

before I knew it, I had thorns and weeds all around me

my heart was overgrown and unhappy

yet you still sought to be pleased

GIVE

I gave my heart to you

every last piece wrapped up in a box

I gave you my love and my mind

I shared my interest and passions

I gave you everything of mine so that you would have everything

    for yourself

you took it all and snatched it up before I could even hand it to you

you were never satisfied, always wanted more

I kept picking myself apart

finding a way to give you every inch of my body but yet it still

    wasn't enough

you never made me a priority

yet, each time I stood there with open arms

you begged for more and there I was

tiny, broken, and sore

I had no more- I gave you all of me and you just walked away as if I
was nothing

Your hands were always warm,

whenever I was cold all I needed was your touch

a hand on my shoulder, the other placed in my own

one touch from you and I knew everything would be okay

I let you climb into my body

up the vines, through the leaves

you dug into my roots, took as you pleased

I gave you more as I continued to grow

shared my all until I was no more.

I let you climb into my body

up the vines, through the leaves

you dug into my roots, took as you pleased

I gave you more as I continued to grow

shared my all until I was no more.

Our minds tend to drift into alternative realities before facing our perspectives on the real world.

You placed me on a pedestal

told me my job was to take care of everyone

if I didn't, they would crumble beneath my feet

a message struck through my head, written in stone

I took to heart and made it a goal;

the foundation is what I became

but for them, it was all a game

the golden child is my name

We tend to gravitate to the things we know are not good for us

left with a temporary feeling of bliss

whether it is material objects or toxic highs

we fuel our bodies with people who hurt us, making it hard to ever

fully get away

we hold onto the bad when we know we will be okay without it in

the end

the feeling of uncertainty creeps around the corner

it lurks, waiting for us to decide what we want

yet all the choices we make are all but permanent

because nothing real lasts forever

People are constantly wanting everything they don't have.

they have trouble realizing that everything they need is right in

front of them.

K.J. Bashford

HURT

The night sits heavily on my body, suffocating me

wisps of smoke file in and out between my lips

my breath smells of liquor

the man behind me kisses me softly, tasting me

I want to run, but my emotions have stopped me

I can't leave this haven

there is a curse that runs through my veins

my body pulses as it shoots through me

I want to feel alive, to be forever young

-why won't anyone stop me?

K.J. Bashford

Our bodies hung over like weeping willows

bottles stacked on one another, the poison filling our bodies

stomachs twisted in knots

tongues tied up together like shoelaces that have been double

    knotted since third grade gym class

we sway side by side hoping to catch each other before we fall

    searching for a new drug to find a new high

we want to fill the empty mind with more worthless thoughts;

our eyes become glossy as we slowly seep into each other souls

sinking, drowning, gasping for more as we die down

    -what is it that we want?

the love, the lust, the loss,

the drugs, the pain, the high,

spiraling and spinning out of control

we hold each other thinking we are all that we have

I've become so tangled up in your words I can't even find my own

I feel lost and broken and sore, but yet my body yearns for more

you are my drug that became mindful for food for my soul

13

Flowers from my heart

a curse and blessing tied into one and yet we are both in this just

for the fun

"Trust me. I got you." He said.

had my heart dangling by a thread.

you let me fall into a hole you dug for me.

a hit to the mind

a stab to the heart

a beat down on my body

You swept me off my feet

gave me the attention we all crave at some point

long days and nights talking late upon the moonlight

our bodies lying low but our hearts strung high

    we were on the highs of love

not falling in love but feeding off of that sickening feeling that is all but

    real

a liking to you, I took by hand

leaning into you, feeling secure

you were just a tease, morphed into something you thought would please

    me

pretended you cared

sharing thoughts and exchanging ideas

they were all a scheme just to get inside me.

you opened me up, broke me apart with your dirty soul

kissed me like it would last an eternity

the connection we wanted was all a mystery played out on a different

    wavelength

setting sail to something out beyond

Flowers from my heart

you drew me in, the water pulled in all directions

I felt my lungs fill up

your personality suffocated me

you tossed me around like a puppet, swung back and forth until you were

   happy

leaving me worn and hung out to dry

despite being fooled, I hold no anger towards you

we possess many feelings but only choose to express the ones that

   affect us most

you picked out something you didn't like about me, said it bothered you.

all an excuse to get rid of me and my body

you take down all those innocent pretty girls that cross your path

it is not our fault for getting caught up in your games

let us learn from our past- funny thing is that you know this mistake

   won't be your last

as time passed by, you left me mute and unspoken

I felt like total shit.

although the difference between you and I is that I will progress and

move past this, but you will continue you.

you are the fool who really made the mistake

impulse fed into our veins pushing us into the fast lane

hard to resist but a terrible act to want to persist

you won't change but only progress into the ugly mess you already

    possess

He decided to keep me even though I left a long time ago.

You keep praying that I'll come back to you

    you are just a fool

I thought you were cool, walking up to me with your hair pulled

    back and sunglasses on.

I saw my reflection in the lenses

for a quick second, I said to myself "oh shit."

I must cleanse myself

feel myself, forget you and heal myself

for I am the only one for me

you can't see that because you are too wrapped up in yourself

you are a disaster

calling me a ball of stress, when I'm over here confessing to you
that you are the one in distress

shit.

you grab a cigarette, hands around my neck

telling me I can't leave

reality check, you were the one who lacked in our entanglement

You came at me like a vulture looking for fresh meat

soreness hits in between my legs

my body aches with discomfort and pain

you swing your shit around meanwhile you can't even see what is

good for yourself

You mixed trust into lust, lacking love.

Confusion laid upon my lips as you planted yours onto mine

hands pressed into my body, I felt uneasy

you placed more pressure onto me

I couldn't see your face

my eyes hardly awake

out from under came my pants

I lay half-nude upon your presence

without any regard in you went

pushing with all of your might

mute was all I could be

one, two, three…until I screamed

"no." this isn't what I want

you stopped, pulled back in disgust

my voice was heard

I think we were both in shock

you lifted me up from the ground

tears ran down my face as I sought comfort

but you stood there

confusion struck again this time on your lips

dawned upon what just happened and what went wrong

miscommunication flew through the room

I got up, turned around, and left you

I was so suppressed from you that I didn't even know who I was

anymore.

Through the screen door is what we seek

a quick peek perhaps is all we need

gossip slips in and out while hurtful words slowly creep about

tiny pixels to make up a fake world

we stop and glare at others who are just as unaware that this

    place is only to disrespect one another

climb to the top of the feed only to reach that unsatisfactory once

    again

our eyes sunken into the screen, drooping and dripping as far as

    we can see

quickly bouncing from one picture to the next

only to be entertained for a matter of seconds

body after body we gaze upon

undress, redress, each Barbie we see is caught up in her own

mess

there are two faces, only one glows

as the ugly side sits back in despair

we post images to please others, hardly ourselves

each like that strikes makes our minds scream

tiny hits of dopamine fill our veins as we shoot them up

    we pulse

    we shout

    we feel

feel what though?

a temporary happiness and addiction to something that isn't real?

it is only ourselves who can fulfill the happiness that everyone

    else seeks

the words slide up into our bodies to feed our starving souls

they wrap around our heads squeezing us to get the reaction

    everyone else wants

our purpose in life is being lost into a vortex of a plastic reality

trash is what we've become and it is only us who can clean it up

we are a society who must disconnect to reconnect

to the screen door, but this time we won't open it

Sweet bitterness looks good on you.

I watched you from behind the door

I held my hand over my mouth

little piles of white dust laid out on the floor

there you were standing there

your face cold and pale

ribcage exposed

trying to take in tiny gasps of air

you leaned down and bent over

I turned my face away

you had two paths, but you chose the one covered with cocoa

not sweet like chocolate, but bitter like the way it tasted when you

    rubbed it on your gums

only you can save yourself from the dangers you've unraveled

your life path was suddenly set out in different lines that lay right

    before your eyes

We get so tangled up in the damage that we forget how to love.

You mumbled something from the corner of your mouth

stared at me from across the room

my eyes narrowed in as I began to focus on you

I looked at you, trying to figure out what to say

I walked my way towards you and pressed myself onto your body

my tear drops stained you as they fell from my face

little ripples of salted water rolled between the layers of your skin

eyes heavy and weary with uncertainty

your mood fell deeper than the temperature on a cold winter's day;

you touched my face softly

your body told me to go but your heart said to stay

our colors don't blend anymore

they turn into the mixture of a dark deep depression

leaving us with an impression of our emotions

that is all that is left to see

I absorbed you like a sponge.

Fed off your bad habits.

My thoughts are consuming me.

Eating away at the little bits that have been left from you.

You never made me feel like a priority.

Your words hit deep into my spine as you slowly injected them

controlling my mind, trying to morph me into something I was not

I felt so blinded by you, I couldn't get away

each day I got another dose of you

your thoughts consumed my own to the point where I wasn't even

thinking for myself-

I came down with a horrible case of you

I lay awake at night contemplating if I made the right choice.

Flowers from my heart

Our sluggish bodies slowly shuffled into the bathroom

I flicked the light on, you rubbed your eyes

black and purple circles sat heavy on our faces

orange bottles decorated the white porcelain counter top

labels upon labels and tiny capsules filled with our candy

pop one, two, three.

"wait, stop" you said. "hold me."

laughing and sobbing together we sat

warm water filled the tub, our naked bodies sat upon one another

steam captured the mirror, droplets of water slid down the wall

    you smiled at me with those weary eyes

    and gave me one last look before you said goodbye

You've replaced me several times,

tried to stick new people in your life who you thought looked good

    standing next to you

only for each to do something you didn't like

betrayal, jealously, or a fight-

there I stood along the sidelines

waiting for you to come back

fall into my arms, with tears spread across your face

you knew in that moment that I was never going to leave your side

until it happened again.

person after person, you hoped for more

when all you needed waited here, never gave up on you in the first

    place before

Our love faded away before we had time to heal again.

You had me on edge

hands wrapped around my throat

you held on tight for what I thought would last forever

then you let go

down I went, hitting the floor

I shattered into a million pieces

there I was in shambles

while you stood over me.

I started to put myself back together

but it was too late, I was defeated.

the game was over.

I had lost and you won

My indecisiveness gets me into trouble.

I always end up hurting the ones I love most.

My biggest insecurity is you.

You tried to replace me with her.

I came to you for advice

you shut me down without thinking twice

a judgmental mind is what you've got

I thought you were worth it so I gave you another shot

It hurts less now, because I've known the truth for so long.

We drank until our bodies were filled to the top, but we still felt empty.

You picked apart my flesh wounds

    the same ones that you once marked on me

I kept thinking somehow you were going to heal them

    they would close from time to time,

only to reopen when you struck again

    they would become inflamed with you

but I am the only one who can patch these wounds up

    this time- they will stay healed because you are no longer

Regret sat in between her legs.

Colors bled from my veins as you sliced me open

you did not compliment me

our canvas looked like a battle scene

you used me until I was no more

scraped the paint off until I was bone dry

I became brittle and broken

you wanted new and fresh colors

something you thought would make you happy again

You picked away at my body until it was hollow and dry.

You called me out on falsehoods

your mood turned cold and blue

a narrow gaze you set upon me

waiting till I'd crack

it was then that I realized I had done nothing

you hid the ugly truth

knowing once it was discovered that you did wrong

you'd be left out; alone

My heart aches for you, but my mind hates you.

You are so unsettling.

You slowly peeled my thoughts off of me-

to you they were like dead skin,

so, you stripped them for pleasure and amusement

Shadows are meant to be chased after, not people who don't deserve you.

It was just about noon when we woke up

sunlight creeped in between the blinds,

smoke filled every corner of the room, hugging our bodies softly

we sat in bed half-naked laying on top of one another

our clothing spread out across the floor, sheets still tangled up

    from the night before

the day seem to stretch by as we laid there

soaking up each other's thoughts

drinking away the memories by the minute

seemed like we got trapped in another world,

so unclear as to what we were doing

searching for answers that could only be found by ourselves

we laid low like this, thinking it was the only way either of us could

    seek happiness again.

we spit out words

spoke to each other

but yet there was no conversation

We used to laugh together

danced, smiled, and talked with each other

we loved and fought with one another

now I hardly know who you are anymore.

so frigid and distant

sorrow sits on your lips

misery is heavy in your eyes

you don't laugh, hardly smile anymore

    did you forget about me?

I have so many questions about what went wrong and where you

    went- we drifted apart but I never left.

I'm having a "missing you" kind of day.

Damage wrapped around your body tighter than the belt you used

to be hit with.

Her beauty slipped through his fingers before he got a chance to

tell her he loved her.

Her lips tasted as sweet as caramel,

so he took a bite out of her heart

but wanted to share her sweetness;

all he tasted was bitterness because her heart did not belong on

    his sleeve

Thinking about you led my mind into a maze of untold truths.

I kissed you softly as tears ran down my cheeks, knowing this

would be the last time my lips laid upon yours.

Your words swallowed me whole.

I sought comfort in those who didn't love me.

He became her excuse for an escape.

K.J. Bashford

LOVE

The night slipped away through our fingertips

hand in hand we stood

kissing each other in the middle of the cobblestone street

I stood up on my toes to steal a kiss from you,

the way you looked at me was all I knew

you changed my perspective on the idea of love completely

We sat back on the rock leaning against each other

the warm September air wrapped around our bodies as we sank

    deeper into one another

the water around us was calm

the wind whistled in the background alongside the chirping crickets

everything felt just as it should have been

I turned my face towards you

took a moment to really admire all of you

you held my hands, I felt your warmth

your heat gave me chills

a quick kiss on the cheek was all it started as,

sweet and innocent,

giving me butterflies for the first time all over again

Flowers from my heart

Hurt less and love a whole lot more.

Your hands slid down my body,

our breathing was heavy

you lifted me up and carried me across the room

up against the wall our bodies pressed into one another

you laid your fingers on me again

tiny hairs stood up at your touch

we held each other close,

reassurance filed into the room-

a look into my eyes suddenly made it clear that

we weren't going anywhere

Sweetness is pure honey on your lips.

It's been awhile now.

my feelings for you haven't changed.

they've only grown stronger as you slipped further away.

distance became the closest thing I had to you.

you are happier now;

maybe it's better that way.

Our love was perfectly executed.

Grow alongside me rather than becoming dependent on me.

Defining love can be scary, but showing it to the right person leaves you with a feeling like no other.

K.J. Bashford

I blink twice to know you're all mine,

thinking of the little ways you let me know;

a kiss at the base of my neck, arms wrapped

around my waist - my heart is strung high

He does not define you.

She stands tall like a statue

poised as a dancer, caught in the light

she is strong like the mountains

creating waves with the wisps of her breath

she created herself;

paint drips down her canvas as she explodes with color

a body captured in perfection, with beauty and grace,

but her true self shines through her soul and mind

with that, a self-portrait is created

Our love was like walking on a pile of hot stones.

He ran his fingers through her hair that swayed back and forth like

    the strands of wheat in a field

he held her in his arms, captivated her in his kiss

and she prayed for him to never leave,

for she does not seek to be alone

We always had something unspoken between us

I saw the way you looked at me

always gazed upon my body, smiling as I caught your attention

but we never talked about it

one night we looked out into the sky

and spoke the unspoken truth that sat beneath our fingertips,

that crept underneath our lips

one kiss was stolen, but sealed up for good

lost for words, we are mute

and now it is open and left with nowhere to go

Learn to impress yourself every day.

Their eyes met across the room

a silent gaze sat upon their faces

an uproar of emotions hit the floor-

they seemed so far apart

stuck in this crowded room

they made their way through the many faces,

along the way they became as clear as day

they knew this was about to blossom into

    something they didn't understand

To be in your presence was all I needed.

Your fingers glided down my neck,

moved along my breasts,

slipped into my pants, down to my skin

your kiss was captivating

you held me so tight as you moved into more;

we slowly undressed, tossed and turned until our bodies became a

tangled mess

To gain someone's heart you first must find your own.

She is like a work of art-

you really have to spend time looking at her in order to figure her

out.

You took me to this place I had always dreamt about,

an alternative ecstasy

    my mind set at ease

    my heart craving for more

lost in complete madness

your body felt hot as I pressed my hands onto your skin

you yearned for more,

one kiss melted us into a sweet sensation of bliss

Know that you are not alone, love is everywhere.

You matter.

You were like a storybook character that I crushed on since middle

school.

No matter what is going on in your life, someone else right alongside you is going through the exact same thing.

You pressed into me

my breathing was slow

a moment of feeling secure,

an act so pure

If you were with me, we'd light up the entire galaxy.

Our bodies may have grown apart, but our souls have grown closer than ever.

ACCEPTANCE

When I first met you, I was still in my cocoon

you saw a tiny bit of me until I got comfortable with you

I thought you'd be the perfect provider for me

I chose to stay for a while and plant myself-

I began to grow

you always stood back and watched

I felt on top of the world

my wings began to form

until one day you tried to clip them

you wanted me to change back but it was impossible

you didn't like the new me, afraid I would overcome your ways

I tried to fly away as you caught me,

the idea of leaving seemed impossible

but one day I gained enough courage to spread my wings

I had become the butterfly I've always wanted to be

Her beauty was like a flower

she started out small, with just a few petals

from there she grew

she blossomed, her colors were so vivid,

captured in the sunlight

she stood tall and spread her leaves,

she knew her journey had just begun

True happiness simply resides in oneself

things come along in someone's life that they think makes them

    happy

soon to find out that feeling is all but existent coming from

    someone else

voids will be filled, emptiness is satisfied, and loneliness is fulfilled

everything can be fun and worthwhile, but in the end, leave you

    feeling bewildered and lost

we seek happiness in things we know won't provide it

all we must do is look into ourselves and happiness becomes real

I was so fixated on you that I forgot who I was.

My thoughts are like wind-up toys

they begin really wild and fast

then as I think deeper they start to slow down, coming to a chilling

reality

The beauty of simplicity is all but a mystery

we are so fixated on the idea of materials that are only temporary

life experiences are what last forever

there is beauty and grace in things that we can't necessarily see or

hold

I realized I needed to stop chasing after people who didn't value my worth.

You dragged me to the bathroom, said you forgot to put on your

lipstick

we get in, wait in the long line of plastic bodies pressed against

each other

I'm standing in front of the cracked mirror surrounded by cheap

white tile

I felt like all the eyes around me are judging

everyone was looking at anyone but themselves;

acceptance was left at the door.

I thought I really knew who you were.

Then I met you.

You are a reflection of yourself,

don't change for anyone because it is all but possible;

remember yourself

Being in a dark place is so unsettling

you feel suppressed from your own creativity

the feeling of not being able to get out stabs you in the heart

but once brightness strikes, you suddenly feel on top of the world

creating never felt so good

I know I am okay without you.

Trying to gain that perfect figure will only eat away at your mind

faster than your body

Things for yourself:

Devote, find, feel, be, love

I knew it was over. Just the thought of accepting it isn't over.

Empowerment is only in the eyes of the person who seeks it.

We run from things that will always catch up to us in the end.

Don't let silly boys waste your time

you know you are precious

let them wait for you

chase you, kiss you

place yourself where you know you stand

don't settle for anything less because someone like you only

deserves the absolute best

Our palette of individual colors is slowly blending into a society that

is all one color.

Everyone has two sides to them,

they favor the one side that outshines the other.

K.J. Bashford

Her eyes gleamed like crystals caught in the moonlight

her skin glowed so softly as darkness hit the air

her hair as soft as silk as she lay her head down

her beauty sleeps, yet she lies awake

a wild soul and free-spirited mind

 listened to her calling

spread her wings, set out to fly

     for nothing could stop her

she was on a mission to re-discover herself,

to fulfill a dream that was once forgotten

     she was left in a suppressed mess

she knew what she had to do, reaching for guidance,

happy to be free